CHINESE
HOROSCOPES
FOR
LOVERS

The
Sheep

LORI REID

illustrated by
PAUL COLLICUTT

ELEMENT BOOKS

Shaftesbury, Dorset • Rockport, Massachusetts • Brisbane, Queensland

© Lori Reid 1996

First published in Great Britain in 1996 by

ELEMENT BOOKS LIMITED

Shaftesbury, Dorset SP7 8BP

Published in the USA in 1996 by

ELEMENT BOOKS, INC.

PO Box 830, Rockport, MA 01966

Published in Australia in 1996 by

ELEMENT BOOKS LIMITED

for JACARANDA WILEY LIMITED

33 Park Road, Milton, Brisbane 4064

Designed and created by

THE BRIDGEWATER BOOK COMPANY

Art directed by *Peter Bridgewater*

Designed by *Angela Neal*

Picture research by *Vanessa Fletcher*

Edited by *Gillian Delaforce*

Printed and bound in Great Britain by
BPC Paulton Books Ltd

British Library Cataloguing in Publication data available

Library of Congress Cataloging in Publication data available

ISBN 1-85230-768-4

Contents

8

*Why are
some people
lucky in
love and
others not?*

Chinese Astrology

SOME PEOPLE fall in love and, as the fairy tales go, live happily ever after. Others fall in love – again and again, make the same mistakes every time and never form a lasting relationship. Most of us come between these two extremes,

and some people form remarkably successful unions while others make spectacular disasters of their personal lives. Why are some people lucky in love while others have the odds stacked against them?

ANIMAL NAMES

According to the philosophy of the Far East, luck has very little to do with it. The answer, the philosophers say, lies with 'the Animal that hides in our hearts'. This Animal, of which there are 12, forms part of the complex art of Chinese Astrology. Each year of a 12-year cycle is attributed an Animal sign, whose characteristics are said to influence worldly events as well as the personality and fate of each living thing that comes under its dominion. The 12 Animals run in sequence, beginning with the Rat and followed by the Ox, Tiger, Rabbit, Dragon, Snake, Horse, Sheep, Monkey, Rooster, Dog and last, but not least, the Pig. Being born in the Year of the Ox, for example, is simply a way of describing what you're like, physically and psychologically. And this is quite different from someone who, for instance, is born in the Year of the Snake.

*The 12
Animals
of Chinese
Astrology.*

RELATIONSHIPS

These Animal names are merely the tip of the ice-berg, considering the complexity of the whole subject. Yet such are the richness and wisdom of Chinese Astrology that understanding the principles behind the year in which you were born will give you powerful insights into your own personality. The system is very specific about which Animals are compatible and which are antagonistic and this tells us whether our relationships will be successful. Marriages are made in heaven, so the saying goes. The heavens, according to Chinese beliefs, can point the way. The rest is up to us.

10

Year Chart and Birth Dates

UNLIKE THE WESTERN CALENDAR, which is based on the Sun, the Oriental year is based on the movement of the Moon, which means that New Year's Day does not fall on a fixed date. This Year Chart, taken from the Chinese Perpetual Calendar, lists the dates on which each year begins and ends together with its Animal ruler for the year. In addition, the Chinese believe that the tangible world is composed of 5 elements, each slightly adapting the characteristics of the Animal signs. These elemental influences are also given here. Finally, the aspect, that is, whether the year is characteristically Yin (-) or Yang (+), is also listed.

The Western calendar is based on the Sun; the Oriental on the Moon.

YIN AND YANG

Yin and Yang are the terms given to the dynamic complementary forces that keep the universe in balance and which are the central principles behind life. Yin is all that is considered negative, passive, feminine, night, the Moon, while Yang is considered positive, active, masculine, day, the Sun.

11

Year	From – To		Animal sign	Element	Aspect	
1900	31 Jan 1900 – 18 Feb 1901		Rat	Metal	+	Yang
1901	19 Feb 1901 – 7 Feb 1902		Ox	Metal	–	Yin
1902	8 Feb 1902 – 28 Jan 1903		Tiger	Water	+	Yang
1903	29 Jan 1903 – 15 Feb 1904		Rabbit	Water	–	Yin
1904	16 Feb 1904 – 3 Feb 1905		Dragon	Wood	+	Yang
1905	4 Feb 1905 – 24 Jan 1906		Snake	Wood	–	Yin
1906	25 Jan 1906 – 12 Feb 1907		Horse	Fire	+	Yang
1907	13 Feb 1907 – 1 Feb 1908		Sheep	Fire	–	Yin
1908	2 Feb 1908 – 21 Jan 1909		Monkey	Earth	+	Yang
1909	22 Jan 1909 – 9 Feb 1910		Rooster	Earth	–	Yin
1910	10 Feb 1910 – 29 Jan 1911		Dog	Metal	+	Yang
1911	30 Jan 1911 – 17 Feb 1912		Pig	Metal	–	Yin
1912	18 Feb 1912 – 5 Feb 1913		Rat	Water	+	Yang
1913	6 Feb 1913 – 25 Jan 1914		Ox	Water	–	Yin
1914	26 Jan 1914 – 13 Feb 1915		Tiger	Wood	+	Yang
1915	14 Feb 1915 – 2 Feb 1916		Rabbit	Wood	–	Yin
1916	3 Feb 1916 – 22 Jan 1917		Dragon	Fire	+	Yang
1917	23 Jan 1917 – 10 Feb 1918		Snake	Fire	–	Yin
1918	11 Feb 1918 – 31 Jan 1919		Horse	Earth	+	Yang
1919	1 Feb 1919 – 19 Feb 1920		Sheep	Earth	–	Yin
1920	20 Feb 1920 – 7 Feb 1921		Monkey	Metal	+	Yang
1921	8 Feb 1921 – 27 Jan 1922		Rooster	Metal	–	Yin
1922	28 Jan 1922 – 15 Feb 1923		Dog	Water	+	Yang
1923	16 Feb 1923 – 4 Feb 1924		Pig	Water	–	Yin
1924	5 Feb 1924 – 24 Jan 1925		Rat	Wood	+	Yang
1925	25 Jan 1925 – 12 Feb 1926		Ox	Wood	–	Yin
1926	13 Feb 1926 – 1 Feb 1927		Tiger	Fire	+	Yang
1927	2 Feb 1927 – 22 Jan 1928		Rabbit	Fire	–	Yin
1928	23 Jan 1928 – 9 Feb 1929		Dragon	Earth	+	Yang
1929	10 Feb 1929 – 29 Jan 1930		Snake	Earth	–	Yin
1930	30 Jan 1930 – 16 Feb 1931		Horse	Metal	+	Yang
1931	17 Feb 1931 – 5 Feb 1932		Sheep	Metal	–	Yin
1932	6 Feb 1932 – 25 Jan 1933		Monkey	Water	+	Yang
1933	26 Jan 1933 – 13 Feb 1934		Rooster	Water	–	Yin
1934	14 Feb 1934 – 3 Feb 1935		Dog	Wood	+	Yang
1935	4 Feb 1935 – 23 Jan 1936		Pig	Wood	–	Yin

羊

12

Year	From – To		Animal sign	Element	Aspect	
1936	24 Jan 1936 – 10 Feb 1937		Rat	Fire	+	Yang
1937	11 Feb 1937 – 30 Jan 1938		Ox	Fire	–	Yin
1938	31 Jan 1938 – 18 Feb 1939		Tiger	Earth	+	Yang
1939	19 Feb 1939 – 7 Feb 1940		Rabbit	Earth	–	Yin
1940	8 Feb 1940 – 26 Jan 1941		Dragon	Metal	+	Yang
1941	27 Jan 1941 – 14 Feb 1942		Snake	Metal	–	Yin
1942	15 Feb 1942 – 4 Feb 1943		Horse	Water	+	Yang
1943	5 Feb 1943 – 24 Jan 1944		Sheep	Water	–	Yin
1944	25 Jan 1944 – 12 Feb 1945		Monkey	Wood	+	Yang
1945	13 Feb 1945 – 1 Feb 1946		Rooster	Wood	–	Yin
1946	2 Feb 1946 – 21 Jan 1947		Dog	Fire	+	Yang
1947	22 Jan 1947 – 9 Feb 1948		Pig	Fire	–	Yin
1948	10 Feb 1948 – 28 Jan 1949		Rat	Earth	+	Yang
1949	29 Jan 1949 – 16 Feb 1950		Ox	Earth	–	Yin
1950	17 Feb 1950 – 5 Feb 1951		Tiger	Metal	+	Yang
1951	6 Feb 1951 – 26 Jan 1952		Rabbit	Metal	–	Yin
1952	27 Jan 1952 – 13 Feb 1953		Dragon	Water	+	Yang
1953	14 Feb 1953 – 2 Feb 1954		Snake	Water	–	Yin
1954	3 Feb 1954 – 23 Jan 1955		Horse	Wood	+	Yang
1955	24 Jan 1955 – 11 Feb 1956		Sheep	Wood	–	Yin
1956	12 Feb 1956 – 30 Jan 1957		Monkey	Fire	+	Yang
1957	31 Jan 1957 – 17 Feb 1958		Rooster	Fire	–	Yin
1958	18 Feb 1958 – 7 Feb 1959		Dog	Earth	+	Yang
1959	8 Feb 1959 – 27 Jan 1960		Pig	Earth	–	Yin
1960	28 Jan 1960 – 14 Feb 1961		Rat	Metal	+	Yang
1961	15 Feb 1961 – 4 Feb 1962		Ox	Metal	–	Yin
1962	5 Feb 1962 – 24 Jan 1963		Tiger	Water	+	Yang
1963	25 Jan 1963 – 12 Feb 1964		Rabbit	Water	–	Yin
1964	13 Feb 1964 – 1 Feb 1965		Dragon	Wood	+	Yang
1965	2 Feb 1965 – 20 Jan 1966		Snake	Wood	–	Yin
1966	21 Jan 1966 – 8 Feb 1967		Horse	Fire	+	Yang
1967	9 Feb 1967 – 29 Jan 1968		Sheep	Fire	–	Yin
1968	30 Jan 1968 – 16 Feb 1969		Monkey	Earth	+	Yang
1969	17 Feb 1969 – 5 Feb 1970		Rooster	Earth	–	Yin
1970	6 Feb 1970 – 26 Jan 1971		Dog	Metal	+	Yang
1971	27 Jan 1971 – 15 Jan 1972		Pig	Metal	–	Yin

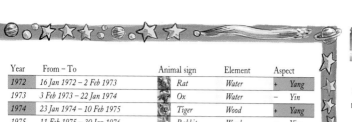

13

Year	From – To	Animal sign	Element	Aspect	
1972	16 Jan 1972 – 2 Feb 1973	Rat	Water	+	Yang
1973	3 Feb 1973 – 22 Jan 1974	Ox	Water	–	Yin
1974	23 Jan 1974 – 10 Feb 1975	Tiger	Wood	+	Yang
1975	11 Feb 1975 – 30 Jan 1976	Rabbit	Wood	–	Yin
1976	31 Jan 1976 – 17 Feb 1977	Dragon	Fire	+	Yang
1977	18 Feb 1977 – 6 Feb 1978	Snake	Fire	–	Yin
1978	7 Feb 1978 – 27 Jan 1979	Horse	Earth	+	Yang
1979	28 Jan 1979 – 15 Feb 1980	Sheep	Earth	–	Yin
1980	16 Feb 1980 – 4 Feb 1981	Monkey	Metal	+	Yang
1981	5 Feb 1981 – 24 Jan 1982	Rooster	Metal	–	Yin
1982	25 Jan 1982 – 12 Feb 1983	Dog	Water	+	Yang
1983	13 Feb 1983 – 1 Feb 1984	Pig	Water	–	Yin
1984	2 Feb 1984 – 19 Feb 1985	Rat	Wood	+	Yang
1985	20 Feb 1985 – 8 Feb 1986	Ox	Wood	–	Yin
1986	9 Feb 1986 – 28 Jan 1987	Tiger	Fire	+	Yang
1987	29 Jan 1987 – 16 Feb 1988	Rabbit	Fire	–	Yin
1988	17 Feb 1988 – 5 Feb 1989	Dragon	Earth	+	Yang
1989	6 Feb 1989 – 26 Jan 1990	Snake	Earth	–	Yin
1990	27 Jan 1990 – 14 Feb 1991	Horse –	Metal	+	Yang
1991	15 Feb 1991 – 3 Feb 1992	Sheep	Metal	–	Yin
1992	4 Feb 1992 – 22 Jan 1993	Monkey	Water	+	Yang
1993	23 Jan 1993 – 9 Feb 1994	Rooster	Water	–	Yin
1994	10 Feb 1994 – 30 Jan 1995	Dog	Wood	+	Yang
1995	31 Jan 1995 – 18 Feb 1996	Pig	Wood	–	Yin
1996	19 Feb 1996 – 7 Feb 1997	Rat	Fire	+	Yang
1997	8 Feb 1997 – 27 Jan 1998	Ox	Fire	–	Yin
1998	28 Jan 1998 – 15 Feb 1999	Tiger	Earth	+	Yang
1999	16 Feb 1999 – 4 Feb 2000	Rabbit	Earth	–	Yin
2000	5 Feb 2000 – 23 Jan 2001	Dragon	Metal	+	Yang
2001	24 Jan 2001 – 11 Feb 2002	Snake	Metal	–	Yin
2002	12 Feb 2002 – 31 Jan 2003	Horse	Water	+	Yang
2003	1 Feb 2003 – 21 Jan 2004	Sheep	Water	–	Yin
2004	22 Jan 2004 – 8 Feb 2005	Monkey	Wood	+	Yang
2005	9 Feb 2005 – 28 Jan 2006	Rooster	Wood	–	Yin
2006	29 Jan 2006 – 17 Feb 2007	Dog	Fire	+	Yang
2007	18 Feb 2007 – 6 Feb 2008	Pig	Fire	–	Yin

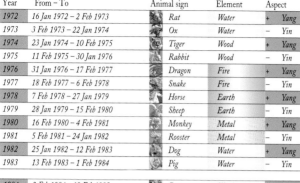

Introducing the Animals

THE RAT	♥ ♥ ♥ DRAGON, MONKEY	✖ HORSE

 Outwardly cool, Rats are passionate lovers with depths of feeling that others don't often recognize. Rats are very self-controlled.

THE OX	♥ ♥ ♥ SNAKE, ROOSTER	✖ SHEEP

 Not necessarily the most romantic of the signs, Ox people make steadfast lovers as well as faithful, affectionate partners.

THE TIGER	♥ ♥ ♥ HORSE, DOG	✖ MONKEY

 Passionate and sensual, Tigers are exciting lovers. Flirty when young, once committed they make stable partners and keep their sexual allure.

THE RABBIT	♥ ♥ ♥ SHEEP, PIG	✖ ROOSTER

 Gentle, emotional and sentimental, Rabbits make sensitive lovers. They are shrewd and seek a partner who offers security.

THE DRAGON	♥ ♥ ♥ RAT, MONKEY	✖ DOG

 Dragon folk get as much stimulation from mind-touch as they do through sex. A partner on the same wave-length is essential.

THE SNAKE	♥ ♥ ♥ OX, ROOSTER	✖ PIG

 Deeply passionate, strongly sexed but not aggressive, snakes are attracted to elegant, refined partners. But they are deeply jealous and possessive.

♥ ♥ ♥ *COMPATIBLE*   ✖ *INCOMPATIBLE*

INTRODUCING
THE
ANIMALS

15

| THE HORSE | ♥ ♥ ♥ TIGER, DOG | ✖ RAT |

For horse-born folk love is blind. In losing their hearts, they lose their heads and make several mistakes before finding the right partner.

| THE SHEEP | ♥ ♥ ♥ RABBIT, PIG | ✖ OX |

Sheep-born people are made for marriage. Domesticated home-lovers, they find emotional satisfaction with a partner who provides security.

| THE MONKEY | ♥ ♥ ♥ DRAGON, RAT | ✖ TIGER |

Clever and witty, Monkeys need partners who will keep them stimulated. Forget the 9 to 5 routine, these people need *pizzazz*.

| THE ROOSTER | ♥ ♥ ♥ OX, SNAKE | ✖ RABBIT |

The Rooster's stylish good looks guarantee they will attract many suitors. They are level-headed and approach relationships coolly.

| THE DOG | ♥ ♥ ♥ TIGER, HORSE | ✖ DRAGON |

A loving, stable relationship is an essential component in the lives of Dogs. Once they have found their mate, they remain faithful for life.

| THE PIG | ♥ ♥ ♥ RABBIT, SHEEP | ✖ SNAKE |

These are sensual hedonists who enjoy lingering love-making between satin sheets. Caviar and champagne go down very nicely too.

羊

16

The Sheep Personality

PLACID AND EASY-GOING, life's too short to buck the system. Besides, it's hard work swimming against the current, so why not just lie back and let the flow gently carry you along. If you're born under the influence of the Sheep, this has to be your fundamental philosophy in life. Sometimes idealistic and impractical, what you desire most is a cosy, comfortable life, cushioned from strife and protected from all the hardship and ills of the world.

SHEEP FACTS

Eighth in order ★ *Chinese name – Yang* ★ *Sign of the Arts*
★ *Hour – 1PM–2.59 PM* ★ *Month – July* ★
★ *Western counterpart – Cancer* ★

CHARACTERISTICS

♥ *Artistry* ♥ *Culture* ♥ *Kindness* ♥ *Gentleness*
♥ *Intelligence* ♥ *Sensitivity*

✖ *Fussiness* ✖ *Self-indulgence* ✖ *Dependence*
✖ *Sulkiness* ✖ *Insecurity* ✖ *Ingratiation*

Sheep hold those close to them in a secure and loving embrace.

YIN NATURE

Essentially, the underlying principles of your sign are all to do with the *anima*, the 'feminine' or Yin side of our nature, that part of us that instinctively urges us to care and nurture, to garner and provide, to love and to cherish. Whether you're male or female, if you're part of this clan, your basic response is passive and receptive. Kind and considerate, gentle and peace-loving, all forms of confrontation, aggression or violence are abhorrent to you.

ARTISTIC SHEEP

Apart from your strong humanitarian inclinations, your creative eye has you towering head and shoulders above the rest. You have an artistic sensitivity which draws you to the world of music and the Arts. Polished, cultured and well-mannered, you're a civilizing influence to all around.

Sheep tread the boards with artistic skill and flair.

18

Your Hour of Birth

WHILE YOUR YEAR OF BIRTH describes your fundamental character, the Animal governing the actual hour in which you were born describes your outer temperament, how people see you or the picture you present to the outside world. Note that each Animal rules over two consecutive hours. Also note that these are GMT standard times and that adjustments need to be made if you were born during Summer or daylight saving time.

11PM – 12.59AM ★ RAT

Pleasant, sociable, easy to get on with. An active, confident, busy person – and a bit of a busybody to boot.

5AM – 6.59AM ★ RABBIT

You're sensitive and shy and don't project your real self to the world. You feel you have to put on an act to please others.

1AM – 2.59AM ★ OX

Level-headed and down-to-earth, you come across as knowledgeable and reliable – sometimes, though, a bit biased.

7AM – 8.59AM ★ DRAGON

Independent and interesting, you present a picture of someone who is quite out of the ordinary.

3AM – 4.59AM ★ TIGER

Enthusiastic and self-assured, people see you as a strong and positive personality – at times a little over-exuberant.

9AM – 10.59AM ★ SNAKE

You can be a bit difficult to fathom and, because you appear so controlled, people either take to you instantly, or not at all.

11AM – 12.59PM ★ HORSE

Open, cheerful and happy-go-lucky is the picture you always put across to others. You're an extrovert and it generally shows.

 5PM – 6.59PM ★ ROOSTER

There's something rather stylish in your approach that gives people an impression of elegance and glamour. But you don't suffer fools gladly.

 1PM – 2.59PM ★ SHEEP

Your unassuming nature won't allow you to foist yourself upon others so people see you as quiet and retiring – but eminently sensible, though.

 7PM – 8.59PM ★ DOG

Some people see you as steady and reliable, others as quiet and graceful and others still as dull and unimaginative. It all depends who you're with at the time.

 3PM – 4.59PM ★ MONKEY

Lively and talkative, that twinkle in your eye will guarantee you make friends wherever you go.

 9PM – 10.59PM ★ PIG

Your laid-back manner conceals a depth of interest and intelligence that doesn't always come through at first glance.

Your hour of birth describes your outer temperament.

20

The Sheep Lover

As a lover, you're tactile, highly sexed and minutely knowledgeable about how to turn your partner on. Loving and giving of yourself, you delight in the long, lingering sensuality of foreplay and lose yourself in the physical act of making love.

IF YOU'RE BORN in a Sheep year, your biggest fear is loneliness. That's why Sheep-folk are so family-oriented, and tend to have large families. Or they settle near their parental home and make provision for a granny annexe to keep the extended family around them. For you, a loving, intimate relationship is not so much desirable as *absolutely essential* to your happiness and well-being. A strong, emotionally supportive partner is the Sun to your Moon, the Summer to your Winter – the dynamic complement that brings balance to your life.

A Sheep's life is incomplete without a soul-mate.

SHEEP OR GOAT?

You tend to be shy, self-conscious and insecure. Some Oriental astrologers refer to your sign as a Goat and say that Goats are capricious, dissipating their energies by jumping this way and that. Only when tethered will they focus their attention and perform at their peak; and nothing provides a better tether for you than a loving, stable union.

The Kiss
GUSTAV KLIMT 1862–1918

LOVING PARTNER

With a loving partner at your side, you feel protected and secure and this gives you the confidence to shine. His or her encouragement enables you to develop your innate sparkling personality, to believe in yourself, to become a rounded person, witty and amusing. On a bad day, you can be clingy and dependent, wheedling and cajoling until you get your own way. But you're romantic through and through and your soft-hearted, compassionate nature is hard to resist.

Sheep feel secure enfolded in loving arms.

22

In Your Element

ALTHOUGH YOUR SIGN recurs every 12 years, each generation is slightly modified by one of 5 elements. If you were born under the Metal influence your character, emotions and behaviour would show significant variations from an individual born under one of the other elements. Check the Year Chart for your ruling element and discover what effects it has upon you.

THE METAL SHEEP ★ 1931 AND 1991

You like to pretend you're a hard nut to crack, but it's only because you're emotionally soft as putty that you build such a protective wall around yourself. Those who are in tune with you, however, can see right through to your heart of gold.

THE WATER SHEEP ★ 1943 AND 2003

Gentle and compliant, you're content to go along with the flow and this makes you easy to live with. With your aura of 'cuteness' and 'loveability', people fall over themselves to protect and look after you, but if they don't, you sulk.

23

THE WOOD SHEEP ★ 1955

Dedicated, compassionate and empathetic to a fault, you seem to attract an assortment of strays and down-at-heels who need your comfort and support. Your kindness may sometimes be taken for a ride, but more often your goodness is rewarded.

THE FIRE SHEEP ★ 1907 AND 1967

More outgoing and individualistic than other Sheep, you're less likely to lean on others for support. You stand up for yourself and like to make your own way in life. With your strong innate sense of drama, many of you Fire Sheep gravitate towards the performing Arts.

THE EARTH SHEEP ★ 1919 AND 1979

The Earth element makes you industrious, independent and resourceful – but also self-indulgent. Your family is the most important aspect of your life and you work hard for the good of those you love. While prudent and conventional, you are, nevertheless, blessed with a sunny disposition.

SHEEP

24

*The right
partner
can lead
a Sheep to
exhilarating
new pastures.*

*Rencontre
du Soir
(detail)*
THEOPHILE-
ALEXANDRE
STEINLEN
1859–1923

Partners in Love

THE CHINESE are very definite about which
animals are compatible with each other and which
are antagonistic. So find out if you're truly suited to
your partner.

SHEEP + RAT ★ *An
up-hill struggle at times though
you could make it work with a bit
of goodwill.*

SHEEP + DRAGON ★
*Despite the sexual attraction,
you're temperamentally unsuited to
each other.*

SHEEP + OX ★ *Your
bodies may meet but your minds
won't and your hearts never will.*

SHEEP + TIGER ★ *Lots
of respect but too much treading on
eggshells for real comfort here.*

SHEEP + SNAKE ★
Terrific friends and sexy lovers.

SHEEP + RABBIT ★
*True love, shared interests, lots of
understanding, great respect.
You've got the lot!*

SHEEP + HORSE ★
*Attraction at first sight is followed
by galvanic passion and desire.
This union is for keeps.*

25

LOVE PARTNERS AT A GLANCE

Sheep with:	Tips on Togetherness	Compatibility
Rat	at odds	♥
Ox	in your dreams!	♥
Tiger	work, yes – marriage, no	♥♥
Rabbit	blissful	♥♥♥♥
Dragon	depends – either heaven or hell	♥♥
Snake	deeply satisfying	♥♥♥♥
Horse	made for each other	♥♥♥♥
Sheep	recipe for success	♥♥♥
Monkey	learn from each other	♥♥
Rooster	touch and go	♥
Dog	a clash of personalities	♥
Pig	champagne and caviar	♥♥♥♥

COMPATIBILITY RATINGS:
♥ *conflict* ♥♥ *work at it* ♥♥♥ *strong sexual attraction* ♥♥♥♥ *heavenly!*

SHEEP + SHEEP ★
You're a couple of hedonists who understand each other perfectly.

Eiaha chipa
PAUL GAUGUIN 1848–1903

SHEEP + MONKEY ★
Very different people, but you could make a go of it by pooling resources.

SHEEP + ROOSTER ★
Difficulties at every turn give only average ratings for this union.

SHEEP + DOG ★
A tiresome togetherness.

SHEEP + PIG ★ *Plenty of understanding and mutual love make this a winning team.*

Christobel finds Geraldine (detail)
WILLIAM GERSHAM COLLINGWOOD
1854–1932

Hot Dates

IF YOU'RE DATING someone for the first time, taking your partner out for a special occasion or simply wanting to re-ignite that flame of passion between you, it helps to understand what would please that person most.

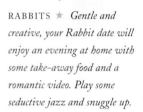

RATS ★ *Wine and dine him or take her to a party. Do something on impulse… go to the races or take a flight in a hot air balloon.*

OXEN ★ *Go for a drive in the country and drop in on a stately home. Visit an art gallery or antique shops. Then have an intimate dinner à deux.*

So glad to see you…
COCA-COLA 1945

TIGERS ★ *Tigers thrive on excitement so go clay-pigeon shooting, Formula One racing or challenge each other to a Quasar dual. A date at the theatre will put stars in your Tiger's eyes.*

RABBITS ★ *Gentle and creative, your Rabbit date will enjoy an evening at home with some take-away food and a romantic video. Play some seductive jazz and snuggle up.*

DRAGONS ★ *Mystery and magic will thrill your Dragon date. Take in a son et lumière show or go to a carnival. Or drive to the coast and sink your toes in the sand as the sun sets.*

SNAKES ★ *Don't do anything too active – these creatures like to take life slooooowly. Hire a row-boat for a long, lazy ride down the river. Give a soothing massage, then glide into a sensual jacuzzi together.*

The Carnival
GASTON-DOIN 19/20TH CENTURY

羊

27

HORSES ★ *Your zany Horse gets easily bored. Take her on a mind-spinning tour of the local attractions. Surprise him with tickets to a musical show. Whatever you do, keep them guessing.*

SHEEP ★ *These folk adore the Arts so visit a museum, gallery or poetry recital. Go to a concert, the ballet, or the opera.*

MONKEYS ★ *The fantastical appeals to this partner, so go to a fancy-dress party or a masked ball, a laser light show or a sci-fi movie.*

ROOSTERS ★ *Grand gestures will impress your Rooster. Escort her to a film première or him to a formal engagement. Dressing up will place this date in seventh heaven.*

DOGS ★ *A cosy dinner will please this most unassuming of partners more than any social occasion. Chatting and story telling will ensure a close understanding.*

PIGS ★ *Arrange a slap-up meal or a lively party, or cruise through the shopping mall. Shopping is one of this partner's favourite hobbies!*

*Detail from
Chinese
Marriage
Ceremony*
CHINESE
PAINTING

Year of Commitment

 CAN THE YEAR in which you marry (or make a firm commitment to live together) have any influence upon your marital relationship or the life you and your partner forge together? According to the Orientals, it certainly can. Whether your marriage is fiery, gentle, productive, passionate, insular or sociable doesn't so much depend on your animal nature, as on the nature of the Animal in whose year you tied the knot.

IF YOU MARRY IN A YEAR OF THE...

RAT ★ *your marriage should succeed because ventures starting now attract long-term success. Materially, you won't want and life is full of friendship.*

Marriage Feast
CHINESE PAINTING

OX ★ *your relationship will be solid and tastes conventional. Diligence will be recognized and you'll be well respected.*

TIGER ★ *you'll need plenty of humour to ride out the storms. Marrying in the Year of the Tiger is not auspicious.*

RABBIT ★ *you're wedded under the emblem of lovers. It's auspicious for a happy, carefree relationship, as neither partner wants to rock the boat.*

DRAGON ★ *you're blessed. This year is highly auspicious for luck, happiness and success.*

29

SNAKE ★ *it's good for romance but sexual entanglements are rife. Your relationship may seem languid, but passions run deep.*

HORSE ★ *chances are you decided to marry on the spur of the moment as the Horse year encourages impetuous behaviour. Marriage now may be volatile.*

SHEEP ★ *your family and home are blessed but watch domestic spending. Money is very easily frittered away.*

Marriage Ceremony
CHINESE PAINTING

MONKEY ★ *married life could be unconventional. As plans go awry your lives could be full of surprises.*

ROOSTER ★ *drama characterizes your married life. Your household will run like clockwork, but bickering could strain your relationship.*

DOG ★ *it's a truly fortunate year and you can expect domestic joy. Prepare for a large family as the Dog is the sign of fertility!*

PIG ★ *it's highly auspicious and there'll be plenty of fun. Watch out for indulgence and excess.*

Marriage Ceremony (detail)
CHINESE PAINTING

Detail from Chinese Marriage Ceremony
CHINESE PAINTING

TYPICAL SHEEP PLEASURES

COLOUR PREFERENCES ★ *Pink, mauve*

Moonstone

Jade

Sapphire

GEMS AND STONES ★ *Moonstone, sapphire, jade*

SUITABLE GIFTS ★ *Silk dressing gown, theatre tickets, body massage, crystal decanter, cameo brooch, champagne, sea-shells, peppermint oil*

HOBBIES AND PASTIMES ★ *Swimming, tennis, reading, bridge, food, buying clothes, sleeping, cinema*

HOLIDAY PREFERENCES ★ *You are drawn to water so vacations by*

the sea or messing about in boats would be ideal. Go to Greece and hire a boat to explore the islands. Visit fjords in Norway, geysers in New Zealand, Niagara Falls or the Italian lakes.

Sheep and ships have a natural affinity.

COUNTRIES LINKED WITH THE SHEEP ★ *Germany, Sweden, Scotland, Poland, Czech Republic, Slovakia*

The Sheep Parent

BEING BORN UNDER THE SHEEP influence means that, whether you're a Ewe or a Ram, you possess an innate nurturing instinct that enables you to take naturally to parenthood. You're deeply family-oriented and if you can, you'll choose to have more than the average number of children. Showering your offspring with affection comes all too easily, the problem being that the mothering can too often develop into smothering.

31

LITTLE LAMBS

Gracious and refined, you abhor bad manners so you give top priority to instilling politeness and the social graces into your little lambs from the very moment they begin to gambol.

Sheep parents love and nurture their little lambs.

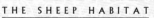

THE SHEEP HABITAT

Traditional is the adjective that best describes your domestic scene. You revel in the conventional role of home-maker, potting marmalade, arranging dried flowers, running up curtains. A strong believer in family togetherness, your house reflects this homely instinct: log fires, comfortable furniture, the smell of freshly baked apple-pie. Male Sheep are also contentedly domesticated. Your décor is sumptuously elegant and your artistic skills will create a classical, timeless look. Your love of ease will ensure that your home lacks none of the mod cons and latest time-saving gadgets to take the drudge out of daily chores.

32

Animal Babies

FOR SOME parents, their children's personalities harmonize perfectly with their own. Others find that no matter how much they may love their offspring they're just not on the same wavelength. Our children arrive with their characters already well formed and, according to Chinese philosophy, shaped by the influence of their Animal Year. So you should be mindful of the year in which you conceive.

BABIES BORN IN THE YEAR OF THE...

RAT ★ *love being cuddled. They keep on the go – so give them plenty of rest. Later they enjoy collecting things.*

OX ★ *are placid, solid and independent. If not left to their own devices they sulk.*

TIGER ★ *are happy and endearing. As children, they have irrepressible energy. Boys are sporty and girls tom-boys.*

RABBIT ★ *are sensitive and strongly bonded to their mother. They need stability to thrive.*

DRAGON ★ *are independent and imaginative from the start. Encourage any interest that will allow their talents to flourish.*

SNAKE ★ *have great charm. They are slow starters so may need help with school work. Teach them to express feelings.*

33

One Hundred Children Scroll
ANON, MING PERIOD

HORSE ★ *will burble away contentedly for hours. Talking starts early and they excel in languages.*

SHEEP ★ *are placid, well-behaved and respectful. They are family-oriented and never stray too far from home.*

MONKEY ★ *take an insatiable interest in everything. With agile minds they're quick to learn. They're good-humoured but mischievous!*

ROOSTER ★ *are sociable. Bright and vivacious, their strong adventurous streak best shows itself on a sports field.*

DOG ★ *are cute and cuddly. Easily pleased, they are content just pottering around the house amusing themselves for hours. Common sense is their greatest virtue.*

PIG ★ *are affectionate and friendly. Well-balanced, self-confident children, they're happy-go-lucky and laid-back. They are popular with friends.*

Health, Wealth and Worldly Affairs

DESPITE YOUR DELICATE appearance and protestations if you're physically uncomfortable, health-wise you're a pretty robust type. What does lay you low, however, is marital discord, because being loved and supported by an understanding partner is critical to your well-being. Should that love be withdrawn for any reason you immediately take to your sick bed; unhappiness just ties your stomach up in knots.

Sheep work best as part of a co-operative team.

As part of a team your contribution is invaluable. Common-sense is one of your greatest assets as are your persuasive talents and diplomatic skills. A brilliant lateral thinker, often you will find ways around a seemingly intractable problem.

CAREER

If you have to don the mantle of authority you will. Moreover, you will carry out your responsibilities with intelligence and tact, but you're not comfortable as a leader and wouldn't normally go for the high status job out of choice. You're much happier taking a supporting role, allowing more assertive types to sit in the driving seat.

35

FINANCES

You seem to attract money which is just as well since most Sheep are outrageous spendthrifts. Perhaps you have a knack with money, or your partner has a healthy bank account, or perhaps you're just plain lucky. Whatever it is, you're always well-housed, well-dressed and, it would appear, well-off.

Highly creatively gifted and with an eye for perspective and design, it's the world of the Arts which attracts you most and in which you excel.

Cash flows effortlessly through the hands of a Sheep.

FRIENDSHIPS

Not the sort to wear your heart on your sleeve, you rarely talk freely about your innermost thoughts. To get to know you, people need to stick around for some time, but the few who do become life-long friends.

SHEEP MAKE EXCELLENT:

Architects ★ Cartographers ★ Town-planners ★ Florists
Landscape artists ★ Art historians ★ Museum attendants
Illustrators ★ Editors ★ Musicians ★ Actors ★ Milliners
Art auctioneers ★ Interior designers ★ Window dressers
Hairdressers ★ Nursery nurses ★ Paediatricians

36

East Meets West

COMBINE your Oriental Animal sign with your Western Zodiac birth sign to form a deeper and richer understanding of your character and personality.

ARIES SHEEP

★ More spirited than most Sheep, you make a brilliant power behind the throne. With an adoring partner by your side you feel you can conquer the world. In love, you're possessive and demanding.

TAUREAN SHEEP

★ Boy, do you have expensive tastes! Security and comfort are uppermost in your mind and are necessary for true happiness. Your talents lie in the Arts.

GEMINI SHEEP

★ Chatty, witty and sociable, you're a brilliant dilettante. You love being surrounded by friends and family but with a low boredom threshold, you can be fickle in love.

CANCERIAN SHEEP

★ You worry about all sorts of things, especially loneliness. Sensitive, gentle and kind, with so much love to give and so much need to be loved, you're the archetypal family man or woman.

LEONINE SHEEP

★ Passionate and high-minded, you have a rather courtly notion of love. You're fun and know how to have a good time: for you, luxury is the only way to live.

VIRGO SHEEP

★ You desperately want a loving relationship but people around you constantly fail to meet your high expectations. Learning to accept others would make life easier.

LIBRAN SHEEP

 ★ Intelligent and refined, you're the epitome of cultured sophistication. You're desirable, highly creatively accomplished and everything you undertake is done with style. Love is seen through rose-coloured spectacles.

SCORPIO SHEEP

 ★ The Scorpionic component toughens the sinews of the otherwise placid Sheep and gives you a more independent and assertive nature. At the same time, the Sheep influence lessens Scorpio's intensity to make you emotionally more rounded.

SAGITTARIAN SHEEP

 ★ With so many projects constantly on the boil you tend to be a good deal busier than the average Sheep. And as long as you're free to pursue your own interests, you're generally happy. Confident, industrious, out-going and tolerant, you take a philosophical attitude to life.

CAPRICORN SHEEP

 ★ Ambitious drive and practicality combine to give you the strength of character necessary to attain your worldly aspirations. Though normally steady, now and again you let your hair down – you're full of surprises!

AQUARIAN SHEEP

 ★ Trying to pin you down is perhaps the worst thing a partner could do to you. You're a colourful character and one of Nature's free spirits – ethereal, elusive and electric. You live for the moment and expect others to do exactly the same.

PISCEAN SHEEP

 ★ Sensitivity always accompanies the Piscean temperament which, coupled with the Sheep's creativity, combine to make you a highly accomplished artist. Like so many gifted people, though, you live in your own little world and the harsh realities of life tend to pass you by.

THE
SHEEP

羊

38

John Wayne

Mel Gibson

Rudolph Valentino

Mick Jagger

Robert de Niro

Boris Becker

Franz Liszt

Brooke Shields

Coco Chanel

Catherine Deneuve ★ Mel Gibson ★ John Wayne
Joni Mitchell ★ Boris Becker ★ Ben Kingsley
George Harrison ★ Geraldine Chaplin
Mick Jagger ★ Coco Chanel ★ Oliver North
Brooke Shields ★ Liberace ★ Robert de Niro
Debra Winger ★ Chevy Chase
John Denver ★ Rudolph Valentino
Franz Liszt ★ Nat King Cole ★ Douglas Fairbanks ★ Cervantes

The Sheep Year in Focus

AFTER LAST YEAR'S FRENETIC ACTIVITY, the Year of the Sheep slows the pace and brings tranquillity to soothe the nerves. The focus is on domestic life: love, marriage, the family, having babies. All these come under good auspices now.

AGREEMENT AND SECURITY

Politically it's a period of reconciliation, a time to heal rifts; diplomatic moves, the signing of treaties and international trade agreements find favour. Commercially, it's inadvisable to launch new products or strike out in different directions. Rather, reaffirm contacts, secure links with existing markets and bring past efforts to fruition.

A BUMPER YEAR

Awareness about conservation and the basic needs of humanity will be raised. Charitable organizations, caring institutions and medical advances will make the news. The fashion industry and the world of the arts will enjoy a bumper year.

ACTIVITIES ASSOCIATED WITH THE YEAR OF THE SHEEP

The discovery, invention, patenting, marketing, first occurrence or manufacturing of: colour photography, the steamroller, the heart transplant, Vitamin B12, the first Montessori school, Mother Teresa's Nobel prize.

40

Your Sheep Fortunes
for the Next 12 Years

1996 MARKS THE BEGINNING of a new 12-year cycle in the Chinese calendar. How your relationships and worldly prospects fare will depend on the influence of each Animal year in turn.

1996 YEAR OF THE RAT *19 Feb 1996 – 6 Feb 1997*

In Rat years you can make good headway both professionally and personally. The trends are very much in your favour and there will be openings and opportunities for advancement. New meetings this year could lead to the blossoming of true love.

YEAR TREND: STEADY PROGRESS

1997 YEAR OF THE OX *7 Feb 1997 – 27 Jan 1998*

Antagonistic elements are likely to thwart your progress in 1997. The Ox is your opposite sign so you can expect challenge on all fronts. Maintain a low profile and shelve ambitious plans.

YEAR TREND: UNCONGENIAL

1998 YEAR OF THE TIGER *28 Jan 1998 – 15 Feb 1999*

It will be a job keeping up with events in 1998 but at least the trends aren't negative. You'll be kept busy interweaving all the various strands in your life but, though at times bewildering, the year will certainly be interesting.

YEAR TREND: SOMEWHAT BEMUSING

1999 YEAR OF THE RABBIT *16 Feb 1999 – 4 Feb 2000*

A most pleasing year in which both the pace and atmosphere are congenial to your nature. Now you can make easy progress and your achievements will bring satisfaction. Romance is highlighted.

YEAR TREND: EXCELLENT PROSPECTS

2000 YEAR OF THE DRAGON *5 Feb 2000 – 23 Jan 2001*

Fasten your seat belt because it's going to be a bumpy ride. Not that events will be necessarily unpleasant, but you'll be expected to sustain the pressure just to keep your head above water. Intimate relationships, however, bring solace and support.

YEAR TREND: MIXED BLESSINGS

In the Year of the Snake, Sheep can charm their way to success.

2001 YEAR OF THE SNAKE *24 Jan 2001 – 11 Feb 2002*

The excellent auspices of the Snake will present you with many opportunities in which to advance and spread your wings. At work, past efforts will be recognized and rewarded. Progress will seem effortless and socially, you will be Mr or Ms popular.

YEAR TREND: MOST SATISFYING

羊

42

2002 YEAR OF THE HORSE *12 Feb 2002 – 31 Jan 2003*

 Characteristic of your volatile nature, this year brings highs and lows in affairs of the heart. The trends are in your favour so you should be able to negotiate successfully any pitfalls in your path.

YEAR TREND: LEISURE PURSUITS PAY DIVIDENDS

2003 YEAR OF THE SHEEP *1 Feb 2003 – 21 Jan 2004*

 Although an auspicious year all round, it's your social life in this, your own year, that will keep you busy and buoyant throughout 2003. The emphasis will be on domestic affairs and personal relationships. If you're single, romance is definitely on the cards.

YEAR TREND: BE PRACTICAL

2004 YEAR OF THE MONKEY *22 Jan 2004 – 8 Feb 2005*

 Monkey years, notorious for their racy, pacy turn of events, are not conducive to your nature which prefers a slower tempo. Consequently, the shifting sands of 2004 will present you with many minor but irksome difficulties and gremlins undermine your relationships.

YEAR TREND: FRUSTRATING MISUNDERSTANDINGS

*In the Year
of the
Rooster,
Sheep can
look forward
to lightening
their load.*

羊

2005 YEAR OF THE ROOSTER 9 Feb 2005 – 28 Jan 2006

If last year tied you in knots, this year gives you the opportunity to unravel all the tangles and make a fresh start. Responsibilities that have weighed heavily or burdens that you have been carrying at work may now be shed successfully. Leisure and pleasure beckon.

YEAR TREND: A TIME OF NEW BEGINNINGS

2006 YEAR OF THE DOG 29 Jan 2006 – 17 Feb 2007

Dog years are generally difficult for Sheep so you're likely to find 2006 a challenging time. Keep a low profile, but do not bow out of the fray altogether. Success comes by getting the balance right.

YEAR TREND: ACKNOWLEDGE LOVERS AND SUPPORTERS

2007 YEAR OF THE PIG 18 Feb 2007 – 6 Feb 2008

A much happier and more satisfying time than of late is on the cards for you this year. At work, forward-planning brings results and a windfall could come your way. An excellent year for getting married or starting a family.

YEAR TREND: BRIGHTER PROSPECTS IN STORE